Disney
Year Book
2006

FERN L. MAMBERG   *Executive Editor*
ALASTAIR TUFFILL   *UK Editor*
ELIZABETH A. DeBELLA   *Designer*
CHRISTINE LEE   *Production Manager*

Articles designed by North Woods Design Group
Stories and crafts illustrated by K. White Studio

Stories on pages 14–25, 36–47, 54–65, 78–89, and all Disney character illustrations copyright © 2006 by Disney Enterprises, Inc.

Pages 14-25: Written by Catherine McCafferty; © Disney Enterprises, Inc. Based on the "Winnie the Pooh" works, by A.A. Milne and E.H. Shepard. All rights reserved. Pages 36–47: Written by Barbara Bazaldua. Pages 54-65: Written by Barbara Bazaldua. Pages 78-89: Written by Liane Onish. Pages 34-35: Art, © Disney Enterprises, Inc. Based on the "Winnie the Pooh" works, by A.A. Milne and E.H. Shepard. All rights reserved.

PRINTED IN THE UNITED STATES OF AMERICA

ISBN: 0-7172-7884-0
ISSN: 0273-1274

Illustration Credits and Acknowledgments

6: © age fotostock/Superstock; © Mary Evans Picture Library. 7: The Granger Collection. 8: © Arthur Tilley/i2i Images/PictureQuest; Brand X Pictures; © Dominique Braud/Animals Animals. 9: Brand X Pictures; Brand X Pictures; IT Stock Free/PictureQuest; Brand X Pictures; Digital Vision/PictureQuest. 10: The Granger Collection. 11: The Granger Collection. 12: © Joseph Sohm; Visions of America/Corbis; The Granger Collection. 13: © Bettmann/Corbis. 28: © Joe McDonald/Corbis. 29: © James L. Castner; © John E. Swedberg/Bruce Coleman Inc. 30: © James L. Castner; © 1985 K. G. Preston-Marfhan/Discover Syndications. 31: © E. R. Degginger/Bruce Coleman Inc. 32: © Jane Burton/Bruce Coleman Inc.; © G. I. Bernard/Oxford Scientific Films/Animals Animals. 33: © Zig Leszczynski/Animals Animals. 34: © Kindra Clineff/Index Stock/PictureQuest; © Richard Cummins/Corbis. 35: © Regina Kuehne/AP/Wide World Photos; © age fotostock/Superstock; © Randy Lincks/Masterfile. 48: © Wolfgang Kaehler/Corbis. 49: © Steve Kaufman/Corbis. 50: © Michael & Patricia Fogden/Corbis; © F. Stuart Westmorland/ Photo Researchers; © Renee Lynn/Photo Researchers; © Bob Krist/Corbis. 51: © Theo Allofs/Corbis; © Michael & Patricia Fogden/Corbis; © Michael & Patricia Fogden/Corbis. 52: © Andrian Davis/Bruce Coleman Inc.; © Patrick M. Lynch/Bruce Coleman Inc.; © Gail M. Shumway/Bruce Coleman Inc.; © Owen Franken/Corbis; © Erich Schrempp/ Photo Researchers. 53: © Fletcher and Baylis/Photo Researchers; © Leonide Principe/Photo Researchers. 68: © Mark McKenna. 69: © Wayne Sorce; © Wayne Sorce; © Wayne Sorce; © Wayne Sorce; © Tony Freeman/PhotoEdit. 70: © Peach Reynolds. 71: © Wayne Sorce. 72: © John Serrao/Photo Researchers; © Superstock/PictureQuest. 73: © Michael Fogden/Bruce Coleman Inc.; © Robert Karpa/Masterfile. 74: © Gary Gerovac/Masterfile; © Richard Hutchings/PhotoEdit. 75: © John Foster/Masterfile; © Lowell Georgia/Photo Researchers. 76: © Scott Camazine /Photo Researchers; © R. Naar/Zefa/Masterfile. 77: © John Chellman/Animals Animals; © Gary Rhijnsburger/Masterfile. 90: © Thierry Boccon-Gibod/AP/Wide World Photos. 91: © Thierry Boccon-Gibod/AP/Wide World Photos; Artist, Gary Torrisi. 92: © Rob Griffith/ AP/Wide World Photos. 94: © Dave B. Fleetham/Tom Stack & Associates; © Mark Smith/Photo Researchers. 95: © Tom & Therisa Stack/Tom Stack & Associates; © G. Bell/Zefa/Masterfile; © James Watt/Animals Animals.

Disney
Year Book
2006

SCHOLASTIC INC.

New York • Toronto • London • Auckland • Sydney •
Mexico City • New Delhi • Hong Kong • Buenos Aires

Contents

We're for the Birds!

In 1905, a group of American bird lovers got together. They were upset because birds were being killed for the sake of fashion. The birds' feathers were being used to make ladies' hats! So the bird lovers started the National Audubon Society to protect birds. Thanks to their work, people stopped killing birds for their feathers.

Feathered hats were high fashion 100 years ago. Birds were killed to make feathered bonnets like this one!

6

John James Audubon

The National Audubon Society is named in honour of John James Audubon (left, top). Audubon was a famous artist who painted American birds.

Audubon was born in France in 1785. He went to the United States as a young man. For many years he wandered the fields and forests of North America. He studied the birds and other wild animals. And he painted almost 500 different kinds of birds.

Audubon's beautiful paintings (left, bottom) became very popular. They made him famous—not only as an artist, but also as a lover of birds and nature.

In 2005, the National Audubon Society turned 100. Feathered hats are out of fashion today. But birds face lots of other dangers. The National Audubon Society is like Britain's Royal Society for the Protection of Birds. They both work to protect birds, and run nature centres with special programmes. The centres and programmes help people learn about birds and other kinds of wildlife.

> Little bird, you are as light as . . . a feather!

Feathered Fact

Birds are the only animals that have feathers. Long feathers on a bird's wings and tail help the bird fly. These feathers are stiff and strong. Short, fluffy feathers on a bird's body keep it warm. Feathers weigh next to nothing. A bird's bones are lightweight, too. Being lightweight helps birds fly.

Hummingbirds hover in mid air while they sip nectar from flowers.

Yum! And don't forget to feed me in winter!

Feed the Birds

Bring birds to your home with a bird feeder! Many birds love seeds and grains, like corn. Put different kinds of seeds in your bird feeder. Then different kinds of birds will come.

Put the feeder where you can see it. Soon a few birds will find it. Then more birds will come to your feeder.

The more people learn about birds, the more they love them. Did you know that watching birds is one of the most popular sports in Britain? It's true! Millions of Britons enjoy bird watching, or twitching, as this activity is called.

Most twitchers carry binoculars and a field guide. Binoculars give you a close-up view of birds. A field guide has pictures of birds. It helps you know what you are looking at. Many twitchers also carry notebooks to record the birds they see.

Birds come in all shapes, sizes, and colours. From top to bottom: a parrot, an owl, a flamingo, a bald eagle, and a penguin with its chick.

Bird watching is fun. It's easy to get started. Just look around. Birds live everywhere, even in busy cities. What birds live near you?

Birds are shy, so you must be quiet and patient. But watching beautiful birds is worth the effort. Look carefully. You may be surprised at how many different kinds of birds you see!

Feathered Fact

At night, most birds sleep in a safe place such as a tree or bush. Most birds don't see well in the dark. They fly at night only if they must. But owls and a few other birds rest during the day and come out at night.

BENJAMIN FRANKLIN

Happy 300th Birthday, Ben!

The Man Who Could Do Anything

Benjamin Franklin was one of the founders of the United States. He was also one of the cleverest people in history. He was a scientist. . .an inventor. . .a writer. . . a businessman. Ben could do anything!

In 2006, we are celebrating the 300th anniversary of Ben Franklin's birth. He was born on January 17, 1706, in Boston, Massachusetts. In those days Massachusetts was one of 13 British colonies in America.

Ben Franklin wrote, "Never leave that till tomorrow which you can do today." And he did a lot!

Ben was one of 17 children in his family. Like most children in colonial days, he didn't spend much time at school. He went to work for his father, a candle maker, when he was 10 years old. Then, at the age of 12, he went to work for his brother James, a printer.

Ben learned the printing trade. But James was a hard boss. So when Ben was 17, he ran away. He travelled to Philadelphia, Pennsylvania. Within a few years, he had his own printing shop. He also started a newspaper, the *Pennsylvania Gazette*. He worked very hard to make his business successful, and he soon became wealthy.

When Ben was 42, he retired from printing. Now he had time for other things. And there were lots of things he wanted to do. Ben was interested in everything!

Ben Says . . .

In colonial days everybody read books called almanacs. Ben Franklin published his own almanac, and called it *Poor Richard's Almanack*. It was filled with little sayings and pieces of advice. We still use lots of these sayings. In fact, Mickey is using one here!

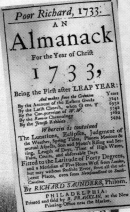

Poor Richard, 1733.
AN
Almanack
For the Year of Chrift
1733,

Early to bed and early to rise, makes a man healthy, wealthy, and wise.

Ben Flies a Kite

Benjamin Franklin was fascinated by electricity. He was the first person to prove that lightning is a form of electricity. He flew a kite high in the air during a thunderstorm. Electricity from a bolt of lightning travelled down the wet kite string to a metal key that he had tied near the end of the string. It was a very dangerous experiment that could have killed him! But the experiment—which became famous—certainly proved that lightning was electricity.

A penny saved is a penny earned.

Only someone who's done something great for their country would have their picture printed on American money. That's why Franklin appears on the $100 bill!

Ben was always working out better ways to do things. He helped start Philadelphia's first fire department and its first street-cleaning department. He also started the first lending library in America. He was the postmaster for Philadelphia and, later, for all the colonies.

He carried out many scientific experiments. He loved to tinker, too. He invented the Franklin stove, which gave out more heat than open fireplaces. He also invented bifocal spectacles. But he never made money from his many inventions. He believed they should be used to help everyone.

Like many Americans, Ben wanted the colonies to have more freedom from England. He came to England as an agent for the colonies and tried to win more rights. He was on his way home when the American Revolution broke out in 1775.

Back in Philadelphia, Ben helped write the Declaration of Independence. Then he went to France. He charmed the French and helped win their support for the revolution. The French support helped Americans win the war and become independent.

Franklin helped work out the peace treaty that ended the war. By this time, he was 80. But his work still wasn't done. He helped draw up a new Constitution for the United States. He died in 1790, one of the most loved and honoured people in the country.

Ben Makes Music

Have you ever rubbed a wet finger on the rim of a glass? It makes a humming sound. That gave Ben Franklin an idea for a new musical instrument. Ben's armonica, or glass harmonica, had a row of different-sized glass bowls mounted on a rod. The bowls were put in a long container. Using a foot pedal, Ben set the bowls spinning. By touching their rims with wet fingers, he played tunes! Ben's armonica became very popular. Famous composers wrote music for it.

That's music to my ears!

Roo's Work of Art

"Look, Mama!" Roo held up the piece of clay he had been working on all morning. "I finished Pooh's gift!"

Roo and Kanga had seen Pooh just yesterday. Pooh Bear was a little sad because he had run out of honey—again. On the way home, Roo had decided to make sure that Pooh would never be far from a dripping-full honeypot. So Roo had made a honeypot out of clay, complete with drips.

"Does it look right?" Roo asked.

"It looks lovely, dear!" said Kanga.

"Can we take it to Pooh now, Mama? Can we? Can we?" Roo hopped up and down.

"We'll have to let it dry first, Roo. It should be dry by tomorrow. Let me get a little plate for you to put it on."

Roo couldn't wait for his Mama to come back with

the plate. He picked up his clay honeypot and hopped after her. Two hops later, he dropped the little pot. Roo picked it up very carefully. A small branch with leaves had stuck to the top, but Roo decided that was all right. After all, honey was sticky— everything stuck to it.

15

"You can put it here, dear," said Kanga as she put a small plate on the table.

Roo put the honeypot on the plate. "Now I want to make sure it stays there," said Roo. He pinched at the bottom of the pot and pressed the clay against the plate. "No falling off," he told the little pot.

All that day, Roo checked on the little pot. At dinner, Roo stared at the little pot. At night, he dreamed about the little pot. Pooh would like it very much, Roo was sure.

The next morning, right after breakfast, Kanga and Roo set out for Pooh's house with the honeypot.

"Hoo-hoo-hoo!" They heard a shout in the Hundred-Acre Wood.

"Tigger!" Roo called. "Come and see what I have!"

Tigger bounced up to Roo and Kanga.

"Careful, Tigger!" Roo said. He held the little pot away from Tigger's bounciness.

"Whatcha got there, Bouncin' Buddy?" asked Tigger.

"It's a gift for Pooh! I made it myself!" Roo showed Tigger the little pot.

"Say, that's a fine-lookin' . . ." Tigger scratched his head.

"It's a—" Roo started, but Tigger stopped him.

"No, don't tell me! Tiggers love guessin'." Tigger squinted, stood on his head, then stood on his tail. "I got it!" he said. "It's one of Long Ears' prize turnips! Yessirree, Pooh sure will like that. It'll  save Buddy Bear the trouble of walkin' down to Rabbit's garden to see 'em." Tigger leant forwards and whispered to Roo, "Just between you and me, I don't think Pooh Bear likes exercisin' much." Tigger winked and patted Roo on the shoulder. "Good work, Bouncin' Buddy!" Tigger bounced away.

Roo looked at the little pot. Then he looked at his mother. "But it's *not* one of Long Ears' prize turnips," said Roo.

"That's all right, dear," said Kanga. "That was just Tigger's idea."

But now Roo was worried. His little pot was already dry. He couldn't change it. What if Pooh didn't know it was a honeypot?

"I want to check with someone else before we take this to Pooh Bear," said Roo. "Mama, can we stop at Piglet's?"

"If you like," said Kanga.

Piglet was out sweeping when they got to his house.

"Look, Piglet," said Roo. "I made Pooh Bear a present."

"Oh, what a very large haycorn, Roo!" said
Piglet. "I'm sure Pooh Bear will like it." Piglet nodded.
"Oh, yes, indeed!"

Piglet seemed so pleased that Roo couldn't tell him
that the gift wasn't a haycorn. Roo looked sadly at the
little pot and trudged away.

Roo was so worried about his pot that he didn't even
notice Eeyore until he nearly bumped into him.

"Good morning, Eyore," said Kanga.

Roo held up the little pot, but he didn't even get the chance to tell Eyore that it was a gift for Pooh. For Eyore just looked up and said, "Looks like rain."

Roo ran off and sat on a rock, hugging his little pot. It looked like rain! How could he ever give it to Pooh now?

"It doesn't look like a honeypot, Mama," cried Roo when Kanga found him sitting all alone. "Nobody thinks it looks like a honeypot."

Kanga held Roo on her lap. "Roo, dear, Eeyore was just talking about the clouds. It always looks like rain to him."

Roo sniffed. "But Tigger said it looked like a turnip, and Piglet said it looked like a haycorn."

"That's because it made them think of things they like. You know how Tigger likes to bounce in Rabbit's garden. And how Piglet loves to make haycorn pies. Don't you?" She squeezed Roo gently.

Roo nodded, listening.

"Well, that's the beauty of art, Roo. Everyone is able to see something different in it."

"My little pot is art?" Roo looked up at his mother.

"A work of art," Kanga nodded. "And Pooh will see something very special in it because you made it just for him."

Roo thought about that, then hopped off his mother's lap. "Let's go! I want to see what Pooh thinks it is." Roo hopped happily through the wood. "Pooh! Pooh!" he called.

Pooh came out of his house, wiping his mouth. His paws were sticky with honey. "Well, hello, Roo," he said. "I was just having my after-breakfast snack. Rabbit was kind enough to lend me a smackeral of honey yesterday."

"Look what I made for you, Pooh!" Roo held out the little pot.

Pooh took it in his sticky paws. "Why, thank you, Roo," said Pooh. "My very own honey tree. And look." He pointed one paw to where some

honey from his paws had stuck to the clay. "There are even drops of honey on it!"

Roo giggled.

"I shall keep this with my honeypots to help them think full thoughts. Thank you, Roo!" Pooh took the little pot into his house and gave it a place of honour on his honeypot shelves.

Roo smiled. A honey tree was close enough!

Rabbit's Rainbow Streamer

Rabbit wants to add something pretty and colourful in his garden. Let's make a rainbow-coloured streamer!

WHAT YOU NEED

safety scissors

string

ruler

different colours of 1.5-cm-wide ribbon

double-sided tape

7.5-cm-wide wooden hoop

WHAT YOU DO

1. Cut 16 pieces of coloured ribbon. Each should be 30 cm long.

2. Put double-sided tape around the inside and outside of the wooden hoop.

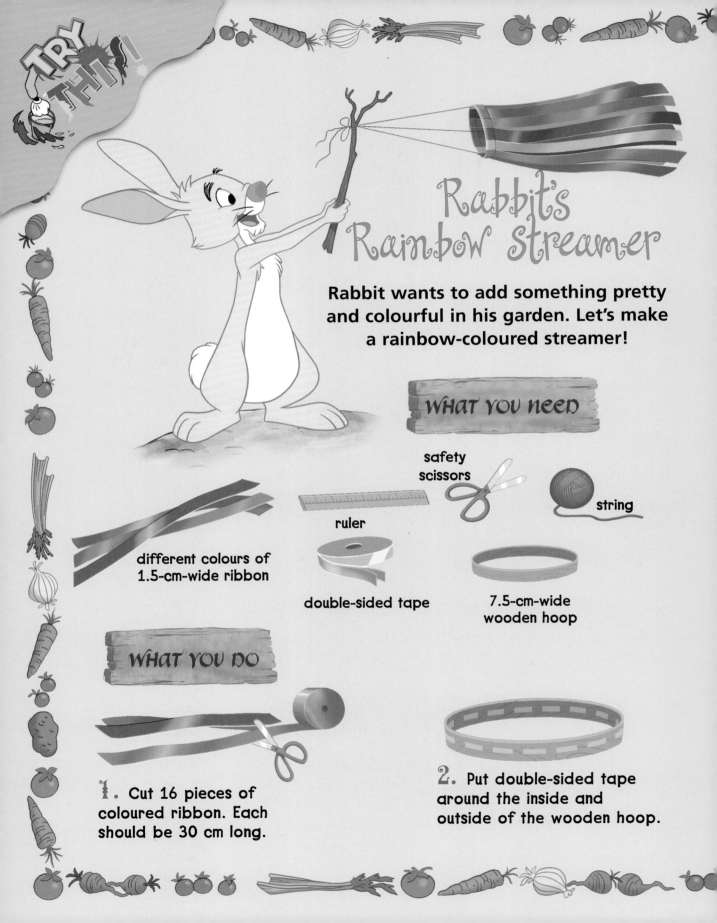

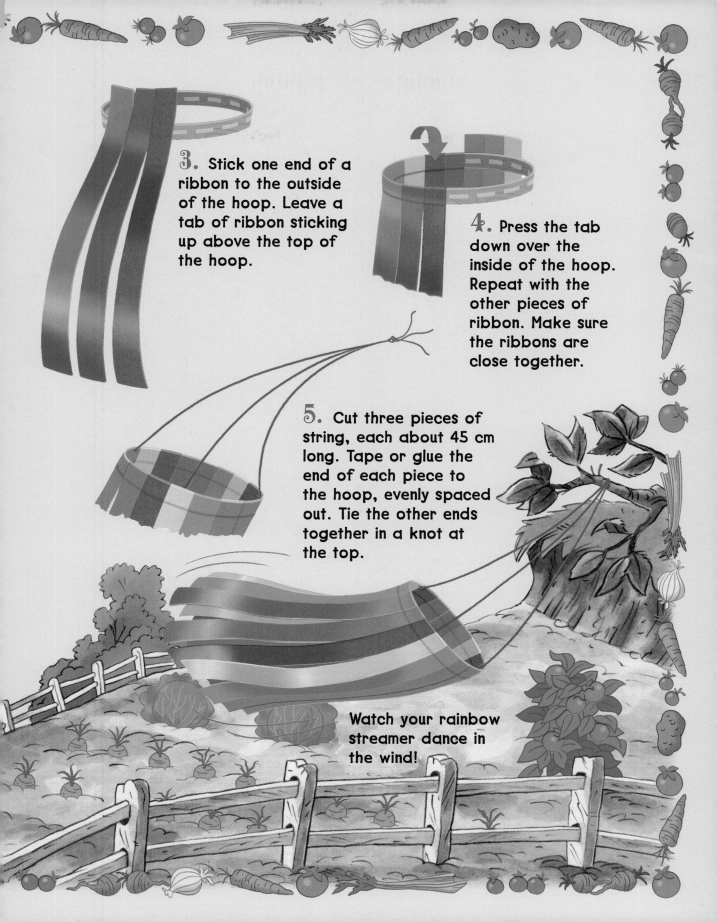

3. Stick one end of a ribbon to the outside of the hoop. Leave a tab of ribbon sticking up above the top of the hoop.

4. Press the tab down over the inside of the hoop. Repeat with the other pieces of ribbon. Make sure the ribbons are close together.

5. Cut three pieces of string, each about 45 cm long. Tape or glue the end of each piece to the hoop, evenly spaced out. Tie the other ends together in a knot at the top.

Watch your rainbow streamer dance in the wind!

Hide and Seek

Look at the picture on this page. Can you find the frog? The frog's bumpy green skin looks just like the mossy stone it's sitting on!

Blending in with the moss helps the frog. Insects and other animals don't see it sitting there. The frog waits for an insect to come near. Then it catches the insect—and has a meal!

Like the frog, many animals blend in with their surroundings. This is called camouflage. Let's meet some of these clever creatures.

Can you find my hidden friends?

28

Flying Leaf

Which leaf isn't a leaf? If you look closely at this picture, you will see a tiny orange eye and some small legs. They belong to an insect called a katydid. This katydid looks just like the leaves around it. It is hidden from hungry birds and other animals that might want to eat it. But this "leaf" can fly away!

Blending In

This picture shows a tangle of dried reeds in a marsh. Look carefully, and you'll spot a bird hiding in the reeds. The bird is a bittern. Its brown stripes match the reeds. When danger is near, the bird stretches up tall and stays very still. It blends perfectly into its surroundings.

Stick Figure

Most of the twigs in this picture have leaves. But one has legs! This "twig" is an insect called a walking stick. During the day, the walking stick hides in a tree or a bush. It stays perfectly still and looks just like a twig. At night it walks around munching on leaves.

Flower Power

The praying mantis is an insect that eats other insects. This mantis is from Africa, and it has a special disguise. Its pink-and-green pattern makes it look like a flower. Other insects don't notice the mantis perched on a flower. But if they come too near, they are caught!

Eyes Can Surprise

This io moth has a double disguise. When the moth rests, only its upper wings show. These wings are brown, like tree bark. They blend in with the trees where the moth usually perches. But if a hungry bird comes too close, the moth quickly shows its lower wings. The lower wings have markings that look like two huge, staring eyes. The "monster eyes" surprise the bird. That gives the moth time to get away.

Did You Know?

The io moth isn't the only animal with false eyespots. Lots of insects and even some frogs and fish have these markings, too.

In the Clear

The glass catfish has a great disguise. Its body is almost as clear as the water it swims in! You can look right through this fish, so it seems to disappear. That helps it hide from bigger fish that might eat it.

Quick-Change Artist

The flounder is famous for changing its spots. This fish lies flat on the ocean floor. Its light-and-dark pattern changes to blend in with the sand and rocks around it.

I think there's something fishy here!

FIRST PRIZE

Another Angle

The anglerfish wins the top prize for a fishy disguise. This fish eats other fish. And it catches its meals with a clever trick. It goes fishing!

The anglerfish has a long spine that sticks out from its nose like a fishing rod. At the end of the fishing rod is bait. The bait looks just like a worm.

The anglerfish sits quietly among the rocks in the ocean. Except for its bait, it blends in with the rocks where it lives. The anglerfish dangles and wiggles its bait. It waits. At last a hungry fish swims up and tries to grab the bait. But the anglerfish grabs the fish!

The anglerfish's clever disguise brings dinner to its door. And that helps the anglerfish stay alive.

Castles in the Sand

It's fun to play in the sand at the beach. And the most fun of all is building a sand castle. It's easy. All it takes is a little water and a few simple tools.

Some sand castles are small and plain. Some are big and fancy. The castle in the picture above is fit for a king! But why stop with castles? Wet sand can be packed into any shape.

To build a sand castle, first wet the sand. Add just enough water to make the sand damp and clumpy.

Next, shape the sand. Pile it up and shape it with your hands. Or pack it into a bucket or a cup. Then turn the bucket over and lift it off.

Last, add details. Use your hands or a lollipop stick to make doors and windows. What a cool castle!

The fancy sand shapes shown on these pages are from a sand castle contest. It took lots of skill to make the big-tusked sand walrus, the sand ship, and the sand crab. But after the contest, ocean waves washed away these sandy works of art. That's what happens to all sand castles!

Look— I just made a sand donkey!

Fox and Hound's Honour

"Hi ya, Copper! Can you come and play?" Tod called from where he was hiding under a bush. Copper was lying beside his doghouse. Chief, Amos Slade's crabby old hunting hound, was sleeping nearby. His snores were so loud, they made his feeding bowl rattle.

"*Sssh*. Don't wake up Chief," Copper whispered to Tod. "I don't want him to follow us!"

"Oh, that old hound dog could never catch us!" Tod said. Chief's ears twitched and he opened one eye, but Tod didn't notice.

"Tod, you're just
looking for trouble!"
Copper whispered.
"No, I'm not! I'm
looking for fun," Tod
answered. "C'mon!
Let's go and find some!"

Copper glanced at Chief, then raced off to join his
friend. Neither of them saw Chief sit up the moment
they had gone.

"So Copper's playing with a fox," Chief muttered.
"And that young whippersnapper thinks I can't catch
them! Humph! I'll teach those two smarty-paws a
lesson." Chief began to gnaw on the rope that tied him
to his doghouse.

Meanwhile, Copper and Tod were running through the woods, finding big piles of leaves and jumping in them.

"All this pouncing is making me thirsty," Tod said finally. "C'mon, Copper, I know the perfect place to get a drink of water and cool off."

Back at Amos Slade's farm, Chief finished chewing through his rope. "Watch out, foxy-loxy," he growled. "Here I come!"

Chief put his nose to the ground and began to follow Copper's and Tod's scents into the woods. Their trail zigged and zagged.

It looped in crazy circles from one pile of smashed leaves to another. Finally the trail straightened out. Chief followed it to a stream that led to a deep pond.

Beside the pond stood an old deserted water mill. Its roof had holes in it. The window was shattered. The mill wheel was rickety, and many boards had fallen out. Moss dripped off it like a long green beard.

Just then, Tod ran past and crouched in the bushes nearby. "Hide 'n' seek, Copper! You're 'it'!" he called.

Chief slowly crept towards Tod's hiding place. But before Chief could pounce on Tod, Copper saw him.

"Tod, look out! It's Chief!" Copper bayed.

Tod looked up and saw Chief standing above him. In a flash, he darted between Chief's legs. Chief whirled and raced after Tod. But Tod was very fast. He dodged and darted, he jumped and leaped, always staying just out of Chief's reach.

"Chief, stop! He's my friend!" Copper called. But Chief wouldn't stop. At last, Tod jumped onto the water wheel and clambered to the top of it.

The water wheel shook beneath Tod. With a loud groan, it began to turn, bringing him down closer to the water—where Chief could jump at him.

Chief crouched, ready to spring at Tod. As Tod came closer, Chief lunged, but—thunk!—he sprawled flat on the ground. Copper was sitting on his tail!

At that instant, Tod leaped off the mill wheel and jumped through the mill window to hide. Chief shook Copper off his tail and ran inside the mill after Tod. Copper was right behind him.

Tod crouched on a pile of old junk in the far corner of the mill.

"Now I've got you cornered," Chief said. He started across the floor towards Tod. Then—crack!—the rotten floor boards broke beneath his weight.

"YEOOW!" Chief howled. He fell through the floor and landed in the mill basement, which was flooded with water.

Tod winked at Copper. "I saw those rotten boards and jumped over them," he said. "Seems that Chief's eyes aren't as good as his nose!"

"Get me out of here," Chief yelled. He tried to
scramble up the rocky basement walls, but slid back
down.

"He's making too much noise to be hurt," Copper
told Tod. "Maybe we should let him stay there to
cool off!"

Tod thought for a moment. He felt sorry for Chief.
He could imagine what it would be like to be trapped
in a place that was dark and wet and cold.

"Copper, we should help Chief," Tod said finally. "It's the right thing to do."

"Well, if you say so," Copper replied. "But I don't trust Chief. He'll just start chasing you again."

Copper sighed. Then he leaned over to look at Chief. "Tod and I will help you," he said, "but you have to promise on hound's honour not to chase Tod. And no crossing your paws!"

"I promise on hound's honour," Chief yelped. "Now hurry! I'm *ffffrrreeezing!*"

Tod started digging through the junk pile, tossing aside rusty buckets, dusty sacks, and bits of broken wood and chain, as he looked for something he could use to help Chief.

Finally he found a long piece of rope among the junk.
Tod firmly planted his paws on one end of the rope.
Then he flipped the other end of the rope down to
Chief in the basement.

"Grab onto the rope with your teeth, Chief," Tod
called. "Then start climbing the wall while Copper
and I pull."

Copper and Tod took the rope in their mouths and
began to pull while Chief held on with his teeth and

started to climb. Slowly Chief's ears appeared, then his nose. Finally, he grabbed the edge of the hole with his front paws. With one last tug, Chief was out!

The old dog shook himself, scattering water everywhere. Then he saw Tod. Chief couldn't help himself. He was a hunting dog—and foxes were what he hunted! He crouched and growled at Tod.

But Copper jumped in front of Chief. "You promised on hound's honour not to chase Tod," he yelled.

Chief stopped and blinked. He shook his head so hard his ears flapped. "Aw, I forgot," he muttered.

"But I promised on hound's honour, so I won't chase Tod—this time." Chief ran off, growling angrily.

The two friends grinned at each other. "Helping Chief was the right thing to do," Copper said. "But I told you, he's still going to chase you."

Tod laughed. "You were right. But you stopped him. You and 'hound's honour'!"

"We're a great team," Copper said. "I think we should call it 'fox and hound's honour'—in honour of us!"

THE MYSTERIOUS RAIN FOREST

Huge trees are all around you. Long vines hang down from the branches. You can hear birds calling and monkeys chattering. The air is warm and damp. Welcome to a tropical rain forest. This is a special forest. It's full of amazing plants and animals!

HOME SWEET HOME

Rain forests are home to more different kinds of plants and animals than any other place on Earth.

Tropical rain forests grow in Africa, South America, and other places that are warm all year round. Rain falls almost every day. A rain forest gets as much as 762 cm of rain a year! That's why the air in these forests is so damp.

The rain helps plants grow. To walk in a rain forest, you must push through tangles of vines and other plants. Up above, tall trees spread their branches over the plants below. Their leaves almost block out the sky.

THROUGH THE TREETOPS

To really see a rain forest, you have to go up into the treetops. That isn't easy. Rain-forest trees are very tall. And if you were to climb one, you might meet poisonous snakes or other dangers.

In some places, people have built platforms high in the trees. Cables are strung between the platforms. Visitors can ride from tree to tree in cable cars, like the one below. The visitors get a bird's-eye view of the forest.

FUNGUS BEETLE

TARSIER

SLOTH

MACAW

Animals live in every part of the rain forest, from the ground to the tops of the tallest trees. The ground is covered with rotting leaves. You'll see beetles, ants, and other crawling insects.

More animals live up in the trees, among the branches. This area is called the forest canopy. The furry sloth likes to hang upside down from tree branches. It spends most of its life in the canopy, eating leaves. The shy little tarsier lives in the trees, too. The tarsier sleeps during the day. At night, it comes out to hunt for insects, worms, and other very small animals.

Colourful birds such as macaws and toucans fly through the treetops. So do delicate butterflies. At night other animals, such as moths and bats, take their places among the branches.

TOUCAN

EYELASH VIPER

Many kinds of frogs and snakes live in the rain forest. Some of these animals—like the eyelash viper—are poisonous. They can be very dangerous. But like all the other animals that live here, they have their place in the world of the rain forest.

THE LEAF-CUTTERS

Leaf-cutter ants are rain-forest farmers! They use their mouths to cut out pieces from leaves of rain-forest trees. Then they carry the pieces to their homes on the forest floor. The ants don't eat the leaves. Instead, they bury them. Before long, a kind of fungus begins to grow on the leaves. The fungus is food for the ants.

BROMELIAD

PASSION FLOWER

HELICONIA

Plants with colourful flowers grow everywhere in the rain forest. But some of the plants don't grow in soil! Instead, they grow on the trunks or branches of trees. Up in the trees, the plants get more light than they would on the ground. Their roots cling to tree bark or hang in the air. The plants get the water they need from rain. For example, the leaves of the bromeliad form a cup that catches rain for the plant.

Vanilla comes from the rain forest!

Lots of flavours and spices start with rain-forest plants. Vanilla beans are the seedpods of a plant called the vanilla orchid. The pods are ground up to make vanilla flavour for yummy ice cream!

Hmm. . . this flower doesn't smell very good!

RAFFLESIA

Some very strange plants grow in the rain forest. Rafflesia has a giant flower that smells like rotten meat! But many good foods come from rain-forest plants. Chocolate, coffee, and cinnamon are just a few. And rain-forest plants have been used to make many medicines.

Today, these beautiful rain forests are in danger. Forests are cleared for mining and ranching. Trees are cut for timber. Then animals and plants lose their forest homes. But many people are working hard to save rain forests from disappearing.

LIVING IN THE RAIN FOREST

People have lived in rain forests for thousands of years. They get everything they need from the forest. They gather nuts and fruits. They grow crops in forest clearings. They hunt and fish. They use rain-forest plants to build their homes and as a source of medicine.

This Amazon boy has learned these skills from his parents. But today the lives of the rain-forest people are changing. In many places the old knowledge of how to live in rain forests is being lost.

Ali Babble and the Forty Sneezes

Rajah was licking his paw after slurping up a dish of smelly fish stew. Abu was eating squishy bananas with his fingers. The two were in the palace garden, sitting on the Magic Carpet and having a snack. The Magic Carpet didn't like having sardine juice and squished bananas dropped on it, but it couldn't wiggle out from under Rajah and Abu.

Suddenly Jasmine and Aladdin rushed into the garden. "Where's the Magic Carpet?" Jasmine asked. "We need its help right away!"

When she saw Rajah and Abu sitting on the carpet, Jasmine was upset. "Just look at the sticky mess you rascals have made on the poor Magic Carpet," she said.

Rajah and Abu jumped up, looking ashamed.

"Don't worry," Jasmine told the Magic Carpet. "We'll make you as good as new as soon as we return!"

"But right now, we have to hurry," Aladdin said. "Caravans are mysteriously disappearing in the desert. We are going to follow the next caravan that's leaving Agrabah, to see if we can discover what is happening."

Rajah and Abu suddenly became alert, and their tails twitched with excitement. They sat down on the Magic Carpet, ready to take off on an adventure.

"You two rascals can't come along with us," Aladdin said. "You'll just get into mischief."

Rajah and Abu watched Aladdin and Jasmine fly away. Then they looked at each other. They weren't going to miss out on this adventure!

Abu climbed on Rajah's back and hung on tight as
Rajah gave an enormous leap and bounded over the
palace walls. He ran like the wind through the streets
of Agrabah and out into the desert. With his sharp
eyes, he could see the Magic Carpet flying overhead.
With his sharp nose, he could follow the smell of
stinky sardines and squashed bananas coming from the
Magic Carpet.

The Magic Carpet carried Aladdin and Jasmine over
the desert. From the air, they followed the caravan
through a narrow passage between rocky cliffs.
Suddenly a huge cloud of dust billowed up between
the cliffs. When it cleared, the caravan had gone!

"Let's go down and see what happened," Aladdin said. But the moment the Magic Carpet landed and Aladdin and Jasmine stepped off, the ground opened beneath their feet. And before they could say "abracadabra," they fell through a deep pit in the sand and landed in a huge underground cavern.

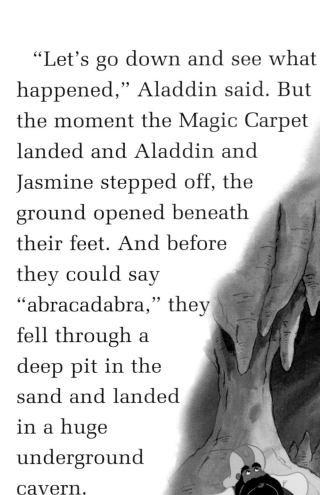

"Ha, ha, ha!" A short, round man with a big red nose and a very long black moustache stood before them. "I am Ali Babble of the Forty Sneezes," the man said. "I made the caravans disappear in the hope that you would come and fall into my trap."

"What do you want?" Jasmine asked.

"I've always wanted a Magic Carpet of my own," Ali Babble answered. "Give me yours, and I'll let you and all the caravans go."

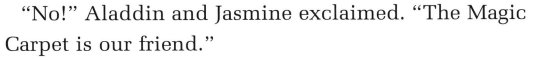

"No!" Aladdin and Jasmine exclaimed. "The Magic Carpet is our friend."

"Then I shall take it and lock you away in the deepest part of the cavern, where no one will find you," Ali Babble replied. But the moment he touched the Magic Carpet, Ali Babble began to sneeze.

"Oh, fiddlesticks!" Ali Babble exclaimed. "This—*achoo*—carpet has cat hair all over it! I'm allergic to cat hair! *Achoo!*"

59

He shouted for his guards. "Lock Aladdin and
Jasmine up," he ordered. "And give that carpet a good
washing!"

Aladdin and Jasmine didn't know how they would
get free or get the Magic Carpet back. They didn't
know that Rajah and Abu had followed them all the
way, and that Rajah was already digging through the
sandy desert floor to reach them.

Using his powerful paws, Rajah soon dug through the
pit in the sand. Then he and Abu crept down into the
cavern. Using his nose, Rajah trailed the scent of the
Magic Carpet all the way to the room where Ali

Babble's servants were preparing to wash the carpet. With one "Grrr," Rajah scared everyone away. Then he and Abu followed the Magic Carpet to where Jasmine and Aladdin were locked up.

Aladdin and Jasmine were surprised and happy to see Rajah and Abu. The monkey found the keys and unlocked the door. Aladdin and Jasmine were free. But they all still had to escape Ali Babble's clutches!

"I have an idea," Aladdin said. When Rajah heard the plan, he purred with excitement. They all crept to Ali Babble's room, where Ali Babble was sitting on a couch, eating grapes and figs.

With a roar, Rajah bounded into the room and leapt on Ali Babble. He rubbed his head against Ali Babble's face. He patted him with his paws. He licked him with his big, rough tongue.

"*Aaaaaaaaaaaachooaaaaachooaaaaachoooooooie!*"

Ali Babble began to sneeze. He sneezed so hard, grapes and figs flew across the room. He sneezed so much his ears turned purple! "Get away! *Achoo!* Get away!" he shouted. "Get off—*achoo!*—me!" But Rajah wouldn't budge.

"Call off your kitty! Call off your kitty!" Ali Babble cried to Aladdin and Jasmine.

"Only if you set us free and release all the caravans." Aladdin said. "And you must leave the desert for ever!"

"*Achoo!* Yes!" Ali Babble said. "I'll do anything. Just get your big kitty out of here! I don't like the desert much anyway. The dust tickles my nose. I'm going to move to the seaside and open a shop to sell allergy medicines. Now—*achoo!*—please—*achoo!*—leave—*achoo!*"

Aladdin, Jasmine, Rajah, and Abu climbed out of
the cavern and piled onto the Magic Carpet. As they
flew home, they could see caravans pouring from
the cavern, and Ali Babble snuffling into his silk
handkerchief.

When they reached the palace, the
Magic Carpet had a long, lovely bath. As it
lay in the garden drying its tassels in the
sunshine, Aladdin and Jasmine came in carrying a
platter of sardines and bananas for Rajah and Abu.

The Magic Carpet flew up in alarm. It didn't want more stinky stuff dropped on him.

Jasmine laughed. "Calm down, Carpet," she said as she spread a blanket for Rajah and Abu. She turned to her two pets. "We must thank you two rascals for coming to our rescue," she said, "but you still can't sit on the Magic Carpet to eat. Even heroes have to mind their manners!"

Buried Treasure

Aladdin has discovered countless treasures in the Cave of Wonders. He is bringing these treasures home for Jasmine.

WHAT YOU NEED

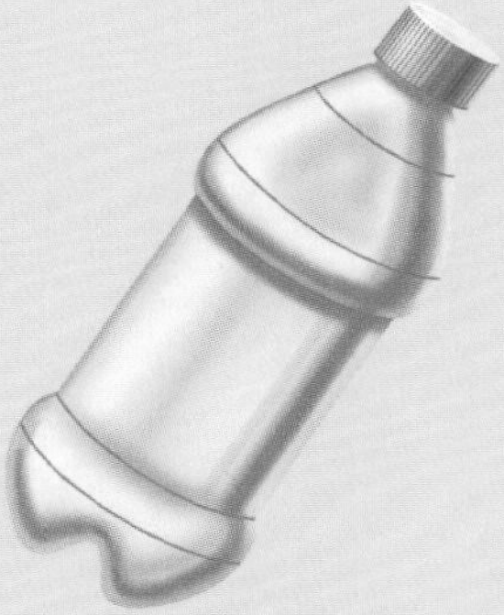

clean, dry plastic bottle

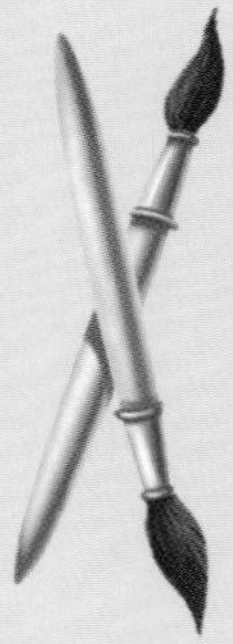

paintbrushes

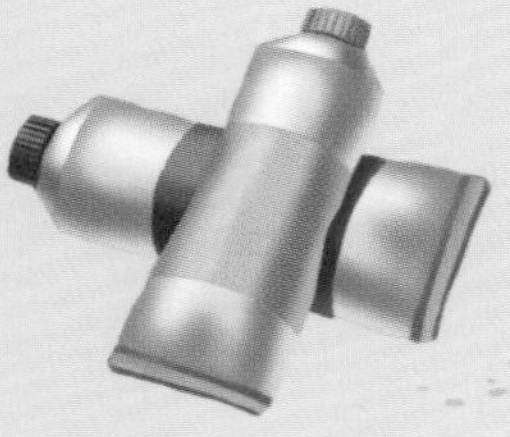

acrylic paints

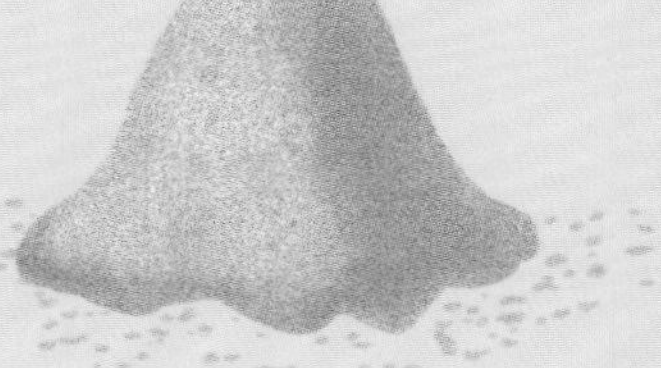

sand

different colours of glitter

little treasures such as beads, gems, marbles, and sequins

WHAT YOU DO

1. Paint a design on the bottle.

2. Fill one-third of the bottle with sand.

3. Add the glitter, beads, sequins, marbles, and other treasures. Place the cap on the bottle and tighten.

4. Roll the bottle over a few times, and see your treasures magically appear!

MAGIC WITH MIRRORS

A kaleidoscope is a toy that looks like a telescope. But when you look through a kaleidoscope, you don't see stars. You see beautiful shapes and colours. The bright patterns change every time you turn the toy. It's like magic!

The magic is all done with mirrors. A kaleidoscope begins with a tube. There is a small peephole at one end of the tube. At the other end is an object box. The box is made of two round pieces of glass or plastic. Between the two pieces are bits of coloured glass, beads, or other objects.

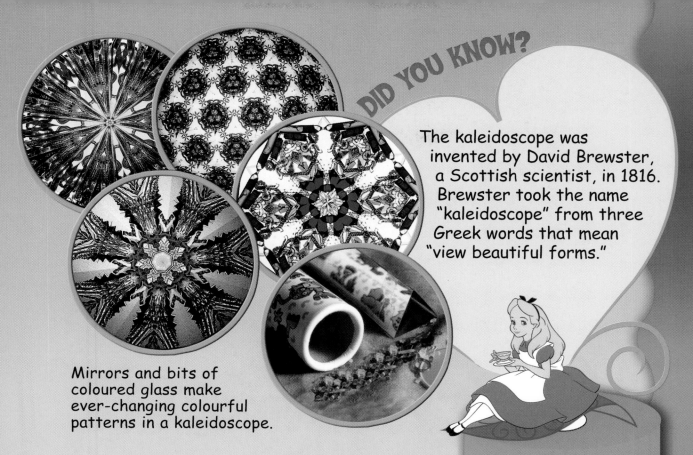

The kaleidoscope was invented by David Brewster, a Scottish scientist, in 1816. Brewster took the name "kaleidoscope" from three Greek words that mean "view beautiful forms."

Mirrors and bits of coloured glass make ever-changing colourful patterns in a kaleidoscope.

Between the peephole and the objects are mirrors. The mirrors are set so that light bounces back and forth between them. When you look through the peephole, you see the objects in the box. You also see their reflections in the mirrors. And you see reflections of the reflections! Everything you see comes together in a beautiful pattern.

By turning the tube, you can mix the objects. That changes the patterns. But while the patterns change, they are always perfectly balanced.

Surprise Your Eyes!

You never see the same pattern twice in a kaleidoscope. There are just too many ways to mix up the objects. Suppose there are 20 bits of coloured glass, and you turn the tube to change the pattern 10 times a minute. It would take billions of years to see all the patterns!

Crazy Kaleidoscopes

balloons

flowers

pencils. . .plus

pushpins

seashells

Most kaleidoscopes contain bits of coloured glass and beads. But sometimes kaleidoscope makers put in other things. Marbles, seashells, flowers, feathers, and coloured sand make beautiful patterns. So do some surprising objects—such as pushpins, pencils, pennies, sweets, and stamps!

In some kaleidoscopes, you can open the object box and change the objects inside. There are even kaleidoscopes with nothing at all inside, except mirrors. These are called teleidoscopes. When you look through one of these, you see whatever you point the tube at. You can look at your hand, your dog—anything. Whatever it is, the mirrors reflect it and make patterns from it.

Wish I had time to see them all!

A kaleidoscope is such a curious toy!

This craftsman is shaping tiny glass tubes to put in the brass kaleidoscope on the table. The tubes are filled with coloured oils. The picture in the circle shows what the tubes look like inside the object box of the kaleidoscope.

Many kaleidoscopes are simple toys made of cardboard or plastic. But some are works of art. Instead of cardboard, they are made of metal, wood, or glass. And they may be shaped like eggs instead of tubes.

They may have extra mirrors inside and be filled with strange objects. Some even have tiny music boxes that play tunes as they turn!

But, plain or fancy, all kaleidoscopes let you "view beautiful forms." They all make magic with mirrors!

COPYCATS!

Who came up with the idea for armour? No one knows. But here's a guess: The idea came from nature. People get lots of ideas from plants and animals. We are copycats!

The armadillo (above) has bony plates in its skin. It looks like a pig wearing armour! The animal's name means "little armoured one" in Spanish.

Rows of plates cover the armadillo from head to tail. If another animal attacks the armadillo, the plates protect it. But the armadillo has no armour on its belly. When danger comes, it rolls into a tight ball to protect its tender tummy.

Long ago, knights wore suits of metal armour for fighting. Like the armadillo's skin, the knight's armour was made up from lots of plates. The separate plates allowed the armour to bend, so the knight could move. Even so, this metal suit must have been very uncomfortable!

Armour— what a goofy idea!

Hummingbirds are tiny colourful birds. They dart from flower to flower, like little flying jewels.

Have you ever seen a hummingbird stick its bill deep into the petals of a flower? What is it doing? The hummingbird is drinking nectar. Nectar is a sweet liquid found in the heart of a flower. The hummingbird uses its bill to suck the nectar out. The long, thin bill is like a straw.

You're such a copycat!

You copy the hummingbird whenever you drink through a straw. Think about it! Like the hummingbird's bill, the straw is a long, thin tube. When you suck the straw, your drink travels up the tube and into your mouth.

This lucky squirrel has found a pile of nuts. But how will it take the nuts back to its nest? It can't carry them with its paws. So what does the squirrel do? It stuffs the nuts into its cheeks!

The squirrel has special pouches in its cheeks. The animal roams around looking for nuts and seeds. It puts whatever it finds into its cheek pouches. Then it takes all the food back to its nest. In this way the squirrel can store lots of food for the winter, when food is hard to find.

You copy the squirrel when you use a rucksack to carry your gear. A rucksack lets you carry much more stuff than you can carry in your hands. But be careful. If you load too many things into your pack, you could hurt your back!

With a rucksack, my hands are free to hold on!

Beavers are great swimmers—and amazing builders! Beavers build a dam across a stream, using wood, rocks, and mud. The dam blocks water, which builds up behind it, forming a pond.

In the middle of the pond, the beavers build their home. The home is called a lodge. It is also made of wood, rocks, and mud. The door to the lodge is underwater. But the lodge itself sticks up out of the water like an island. Inside, the beavers are safe and dry.

DID YOU KNOW?

Beavers cut down trees with their teeth! Their front teeth are so strong and sharp that they can chew through tree trunks nearly a metre thick.

People build dams, too. This is Glen Canyon Dam. It blocks the Colorado River in Arizona. It's over 200 metres tall—one of the biggest dams in the world! The dam is made of concrete. Water builds up behind it to make a huge lake that stretches for many kilometres.

75

Monkey see, monkey do!

This green pouch doesn't look like a butterfly. But it is one stage in the life of a butterfly. A butterfly begins its life as an egg. When the egg hatches, a caterpillar crawls out. How does a crawling caterpillar turn into a beautiful butterfly? First, the caterpillar hooks itself to a plant stem or leaf. Then it sheds its skin. A hard shell forms around it. The caterpillar is now called a chrysalis. It looks like a little pouch.

The chrysalis hangs from the leaf. Its hard shell protects it. Inside, its body slowly changes. Finally it breaks its shell and wriggles out. It spreads its wings. It's a butterfly!

This thick, cosy sleeping bag is a sort of pouch, too. It protects a mountain climber from even the coldest weather. Inside, the climber can stay warm while he sleeps. Of course, he'll still be a mountain climber when he wriggles out. He won't turn into a butterfly!

Look at the fancy fins on this goldfish! The fins are pretty, and they are very important to the fish. Fins help the fish move around.

A fish's fins are wide and flat. The fish pushes them through the water to swim. It wags its tail fins from side to side to go forwards. Fins on its back and sides help the fish stop, turn, and stay upright in the water. Without its fins, a fish could hardly swim at all!

Fish are fin-tastic swimmers!

You copy the fish when you wear flippers on your feet to swim. Like the fish's fins, the flippers are wide and flat. You kick to push them through the water. Kicking your flippers pushes you forwards through the water—just like a fish!

It's Good to Be the Captain

Donald Duck opened the window of the captain's cabin on his ship, the *Miss Daisy*. He yawned and stretched and thought, "It's good to be the captain." He looked down on the main deck.

"Wak!" he cried as arrows whizzed by his head.

"Sorry, Unca Donald," called Huey, Dewey, and Louie. Another hail of arrows flew towards the target that was hanging below Donald's window and zipped over his head.

"Stop!" Donald yelled. "No target practice on my ship!"

"Aw, gee," called the boys.

Donald walked out onto the deck of the *Miss Daisy* and looked around. The deck was filled with pine trees that Donald had just picked up for Daisy's new Duckburg Beautification Project.

"Listen to me, boys. *I'm* the captain! I'm king of this ship," he muttered, banging open the galley door. As he entered the galley, Pluto dashed out.

"Donald!" cried Daisy, batting her eyelashes. "We are so glad you're here!"

79

"Oh, uh. . .hi, Daisy," Donald said.

Daisy turned to her committee. She pointed to the town map on the table. Minnie, Clarabelle, and Horace stood around the map, moving tiny toy trees around.

"Donald!" said Daisy. "Don't you think the trees should go along Main Street?"

Minnie said, "But, Donald, look here. We need the trees closer to the school."

Clarabelle added, "That's a good idea, too."

"I agree," said Horace.

"I think—"
But Donald's voice
was drowned out by
shouts coming from the deck.

"Giddyap!"

"Ride 'em, cowboy!"

"My turn, my turn!" The nephews were trying
to ride Pluto. Minnie and Donald ran out to rescue
Mickey's dog. When Pluto stopped short at their feet,
Huey flew off Pluto's back, right into Donald's arms.

"Wak! No Pluto riding! And no cowboys on my
ship!" Donald said.

"Aw, gee, Unca Donald," said the boys. From the galley, Donald heard Daisy, Clarabelle, and Horace arguing about where the pine trees should be planted.

The boys screamed, "Hide and seek! Huey's 'it'!"

Donald covered his ears, looked around, and headed towards a rowing boat. As he lowered himself and the boat into the water, Daisy demanded, "Donald, where are you going?"

"Fishing! I need a little peace and quiet!"

Donald rowed out onto the lake. The sun was warm, and the breeze was gentle. He sighed. Fishing was something Donald could do in his sleep. With his eyes half-closed, Donald soon had three plump fish in his bucket. The fish thrashed and splashed. Donald was almost soaked.

"Wak!" he squawked, looking into the bucket for the first time. What he saw made him squawk even louder. "I've never seen fish with little. . .whaddayacallits. . ."

"Crowns," said the largest of the fish. "We are the crown princes of this lake. If you free us, we will grant you three wishes."

"Wishes? Wak!" said Donald. He sat back to think. Maybe he should keep the talking fish. Surely he could make lots and lots of money with talking fish. Just then the boat began to rock.

Whoosh! Waves broke over the little rowing boat. Luckily, Donald ducked just in time.

"Gawrsh! Sorry, Donald!" called Goofy as he sailed over Donald's head on water skis. The wake from the motorboat pulling Goofy rocked Donald's  boat, nearly tipping it over. Before Donald could grab the bucket, over the side it went, along with all his fishing gear. The fish were free. Then Donald, too, tumbled into the lake.

"Wak!" cried a dripping Donald, as he climbed back into the boat. No fish, no fishing gear. He thought about the boys running wild on his ship. He thought about his ship. With all the pine trees on deck, it looked more like a forest than a ship.

"I wish I were a king," Donald thought. "Then everything would be the way *I* want it!" And as soon as he finished the thought, it was so.

Donald looked around the throne room. "Very nice," he said, adjusting his crown. "It's good to be the king."

The Minister of Foliage approached and bowed. He pointed to a large map of Donald's kingdom. "Where would you prefer to have the new forest planted?"

The town mayors then arrived.

"Sire, when will we have a new well?" asked one.

"Your Majesty, will you honour us with your presence at our harvest festival?" asked another.

"Your Majesty, our border wall needs repair," said a third mayor.

"Wak!" King Donald sat down heavily as the mayors surrounded his throne. He closed his eyes and thought, "It's *not* so good to be the king. I wish I were a cowboy. Just me and my horse. Alone!" And as soon as Donald finished the thought, it was so.

"Ah, it's good to be a cowboy!" said Cowboy
Donald, patting his gentle horse.

Everywhere he looked he saw nothing but rocks,
tall cactus plants, tumbling sagebrush. The desert
looked, well—deserted. Cowboy Donald thought how
easy it was to ride a horse. Just then, the horse saw a
snake on the trail. Startled, the horse reared up, and
Donald tumbled off. . .right smack onto a cactus.

"Waaak!" howled Donald, his backside full of
cactus prickles. "It's *not* so good to be a cowboy. I
wish I were just me, Donald Duck, captain of the
Miss Daisy!" And as soon as Donald finished the
thought, it was so.

Back on his ship, Donald lay on his stomach while Daisy pulled out the cactus prickles. He looked around and winced in pain. Huey, Dewey, and Louie tore around the deck, this time dressed as pirates. They stopped long enough to watch Daisy pulling out the prickles.

"I just don't understand it, Donald! How could you possibly get all these cactus prickles if you were out fishing?" exclaimed Daisy.

"Yeow!" Donald yelped with each prickle Daisy plucked out. Between each "Waa," "Ow," and "Yeow," Donald thought, "No more wishes for me. It's definitely best to be the captain!

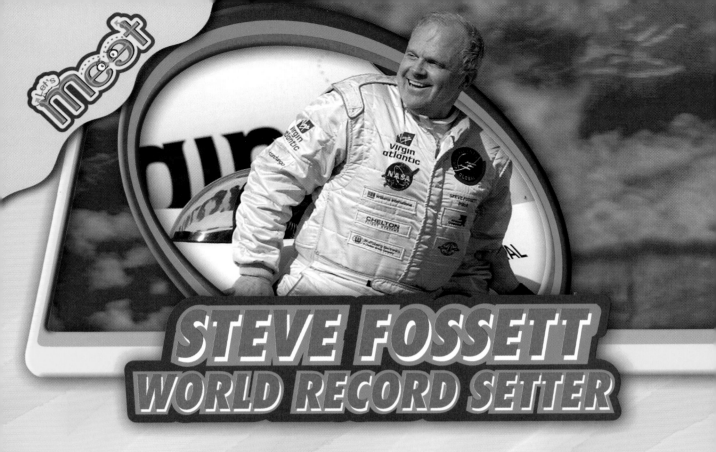

STEVE FOSSETT
WORLD RECORD SETTER

Steve Fossett holds more world records than anyone. He has set records flying in balloons. He has set records sailing boats. And in 2005, he wowed everyone with a new record. He became the first person to fly an aeroplane around the world alone, without stopping or refuelling!

Fossett is from Chicago, Illinois. He likes great adventures. He set the new record in an aeroplane named the *GlobalFlyer*. This plane was designed just for the flight. It was made of special lightweight materials.

DID YOU KNOW?

Steve Fossett holds 65 world records—including the world record for the most world records!

90

GlobalFlyer

- single wing
- boom
- jet engine
- cockpit
- boom

virgin atlantic

N277SF virgin atlantic

Wow! This plane's a one-winger!

The *GlobalFlyer* had one big long wing. In the middle was a small cockpit. Above the cockpit was the jet engine.

The plane also had two large "booms." These booms carried fuel. The *GlobalFlyer* needed lots of fuel to go around the world without stopping!

AROUND THE WORLD

NORTH AMERICA

Montreal, Canada

ATLANTIC OCEAN

EUROPE

ASIA

PACIFIC OCEAN

KANSAS

Cairo, Egypt

Shanghai, China

Honolulu, Hawaii

Calcutta, India

PACIFIC OCEAN

START   FINISH

SOUTH AMERICA

AFRICA

INDIAN OCEAN

AUSTRALIA

Steve Fossett also set a round-the-world record in 2002. He became the first person to circle the globe alone in a balloon! That flight took 14 days.

The *GlobalFlyer* took off on February 28. Fossett left from Kansas, which is in the middle of the United States. He flew east, over the Atlantic Ocean. Then he flew across Africa.

The plane kept heading east around the world. It travelled in the same direction as the wind. And the wind helped push it along. That saved some fuel. Still, Fossett worried that he might run out of fuel. But he kept flying. He crossed the Pacific Ocean. Then he flew over the western United States. Finally, the *GlobalFlyer* landed back in Kansas on March 3.

Fossett did it! He had made the first non-stop solo flight around the world without refuelling. In all, his trip covered almost 23,000 miles. He was in the air for more than 67 hours—almost three days.

The flight hadn't been much fun for Fossett. He couldn't stand up in the tiny cockpit. He had only diet milkshakes for food. And he could take only a few short naps. He couldn't sleep for a long time because he had to fly the plane.

He told cheering crowds: "That was one of the hardest things I've ever done." But it certainly was a great adventure!

What's next for Steve Fossett? Setting records is his goal. So whatever he does, you can be sure he'll do it further, faster, or longer than anyone else!

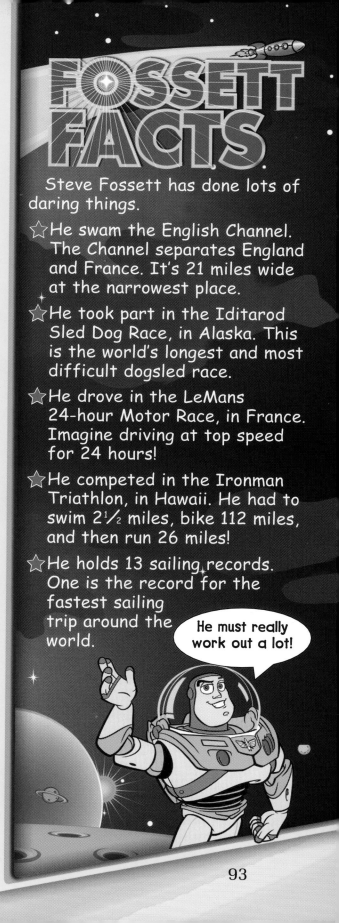

FOSSETT FACTS

Steve Fossett has done lots of daring things.

☆ He swam the English Channel. The Channel separates England and France. It's 21 miles wide at the narrowest place.

☆ He took part in the Iditarod Sled Dog Race, in Alaska. This is the world's longest and most difficult dogsled race.

☆ He drove in the LeMans 24-hour Motor Race, in France. Imagine driving at top speed for 24 hours!

☆ He competed in the Ironman Triathlon, in Hawaii. He had to swim 2½ miles, bike 112 miles, and then run 26 miles!

☆ He holds 13 sailing records. One is the record for the fastest sailing trip around the world.

He must really work out a lot!

underwater

porcupine fish

When I'm scared, I gulp water until I swell up like a prickly pincushion. So bigger fish aren't likely to swallow me!

Come and meet some of my funny fishy friends!

Let's dive into the ocean! The sea is full of surprises. Here are just a few of the strange fish and other creatures you might meet.

lionfish

My bold stripes and long fins really stand out. But don't let my fancy fins fool you. They have long spines that are tipped with poison! Other fish know not to bother me.

SURPRISES

Hello strange fish. Want to play leapfrog?

frogfish

With my lumpy skin, I blend right in with the ocean bottom. I sit perfectly still, with my big mouth wide open. When another fish swims near me, I gulp it down!

nudibranch

I'm a snail without a shell. I crawl over coral reefs, nibbling sponges and other things. My pretty colours are a warning to other animals. I'm poisonous, and my colours say "Stay away—I taste awful!"

sea dragon

I look like seaweed. But I'm a fish—a leafy sea dragon. I swim through clumps of seaweed, looking for shrimps to eat. I blend in so well that the shrimps can't see me coming!

The Last Laugh!

What do you call a flying skunk?

A smellicopter!

What did one maths book say to the other maths book?

You think you've got problems!

What do geese get when they are cold or scared?

People bumps!

Why did the farmer keep stomping around in his field?

He was trying to grow mashed potatoes!

How do you find your mosquito bites?

Start from scratch!

What do fireflies tell their babies at night?

Glow to sleep!

What do you call a doggy kiss?

A pooch smooch!